Christian Evidence Series of booklets

GW01463806

EVID
FOR THE
HOLY SPIRIT

by

William Purcell

Canon Emeritus of Worcester

Published by Mowbray for
THE CHRISTIAN EVIDENCE SOCIETY

Copyright © William Purcell, 1986, 1988
ISBN 0 264 67125 2

First published 1986 for the Christian Evidence
Society by A.R. Mowbray & Co. Ltd., Saint Thomas
House, Becket Street, Oxford, OX1 1SJ.

Reprinted, with revisions, 1988

Typeset by Getset (BTS) Ltd., Eynsham, Oxford
Printed in Great Britain by Tisbury Printing Works Ltd., Salisbu

Evidence for the Holy Spirit

UNTIL QUITE recently, scientists have considered that four types of 'force' were necessary to understand the behaviour of the physical world. *Gravitation* is well known to all of us. It is the force which attracts us to the Earth and prevents us from floating off into space. It is the force which governs the motion of the earth around the sun and determines the motion of all the heavenly bodies. These heavenly bodies are unimaginable in number and distance, yet all maintain their places with undeviating regularity and order through the operation of the force of gravity. This force of gravity extends throughout the Universe and its properties are sufficiently established that the movement of the heavenly bodies relative to one another can be calculated with extraordinary precision as we well know from the recent arrival and departure of Halley's comet.

Secondly, there is a vast range of phenomena controlled by the *Electromagnetic Force*. This is the force which unites electricity and magnetism and in its manifestations touches most of the things we know of and experience. Light is electromagnetic in character, so is heat, so are radio waves and X-rays. As the sun's heat and light energy is absorbed by the atoms and molecules in plants through their electromagnetic nature, it is no exaggeration to state that life on this planet, as we know it, would not be possible without the electromagnetic force.

A third force is the *Weak* force. This force is responsible for radioactive phenomena, so its existence has only been revealed to scientists through the study of nuclear physics in the last 60 or 70 years. The Weak force is an essential element in understanding how our Sun continues to burn and give us life and it is thought to be the cause of supernova explosions.

Finally, there is the *Strong* force, also discovered through the study of nuclear and particle physics. This is the force which builds up the nuclei of all atoms from their constituent protons and neutrons and binds them together. As its name implies, it is the strongest of all the forces and for better or for worse makes nuclear energy possible through fission or fusion. The heat energy generated in a nuclear power station is produced as a result of the behaviour of the Strong force and for that matter the violence of explosions generated by nuclear weapons is a consequence of this force.

It is the long term aim of physicists to seek to unify these four very disparate forces into a single mathematical theory which would explain and predict the behaviour of all the phenomena we observe in the physical world. Scientists are a long way from this goal but over the past few years there has been remarkable progress in combining the properties of the Weak and Electromagnetic forces into one unifying theory.

Spiritual Force
But even as we contemplate the strange and wonderful array of forces, Gravitational, Electromagnetic, the Weak and the Strong, and even were these to be combined into a single all embracing theory, it is still difficult not to be aware of a gap. Most of us know, from our actual personal experience of life, that another force exists.

We know it at the depths of our being, in heart and mind and soul. We know it as a force which gives colour and taste to experience, and which hints at a meaning for life. We touch the edges of it often or, more accurately, are touched by it often, as by a wind which suddenly and at times, for no apparent reason, seems to come out of the unknown and breathe upon us. We can experience this at times of joy and sorrow. We can become aware of it in strivings within ourselves after higher things. We can feel it whenever we are moved to a recognition of beauty in art, and nature, and music. The fact is that beauty in any form, in art, or nature, or music, or, for that matter, in the kindness and love in which people can sometimes show to each other, can all give rise in us, if we allow them to, some of those strange emotions which Wordsworth called:

> those obstinate questionings
> of sense and outward things,
> fallings from us, vanishings,
> blank misgivings of a creature,
> moving about in worlds not realised:
> high instincts before which our mortal nature,
> does tremble like a guilty thing surprised.

So here is another force altogether. We know it exists; because we experience it. What can we call it? We can call it, and it is a true definition, spiritual force. That is all very well; but how can we define it?

Maybe we can define spiritual force by what it makes possible. And here is a very important thing to note. Like the wind, it cannot be seen. But, also like the wind, it can be perceived by what it does. We can see wind moving branches of a tree: we can hear the rustling of the leaves. We can feel the flow of the air upon our faces. But we cannot see that which is causing all this. But that fact does not prompt us to make the mistake of supposing that there is no force moving the tree, rustling the leaves, flowing upon our faces. On the contrary, we know it is there and real because we experience it. So it is with spiritual force: it moves mind and it moves spirit and moves emotion and it arouses the intelligence. And in doing all these things it makes possible a whole range of vitally important human activities. Let us list just a few of them.

First, spiritual force makes possible *creativity*. This is enormously important, because it means the bringing into existence of new and enriching things. Obviously, it is the source of all art, in whatever form it exists. There is creativity in Michaelangelo's roof of the Sistine Chapel, there is creativity in Beethoven's Fifth Symphony, in a scientific process which enlarges human understanding, just as there is creativity in some medical or surgical process which diminishes human suffering. But this creativity is to be found also, and frequently, on much more humble levels. When we speak of someone as 'a creative person' we mean someone whom it is good to know, who enriches life, who has something to give to life. There are many such people, and they are very important.

Secondly, spiritual force makes possible the *exercise of the will*. Whenever you or I say 'I will do this', or 'I will not do that', we have exercised the will; we have not been pushed around by blind forces, we have used a force which is within us to shape our conduct towards the forces which are outside us in the world. So spiritual force in this area makes possible value judgements of all kinds. Basically, in its simplest form, this means the capacity to look at something and say 'that is good', or 'that is bad'. But value judgements of this sort come to life when they are applied to actual instances.

A news story, for example, of gross child neglect moves us

to feelings of anger and revulsion. On the other hand, some report of brave or unselfish conduct has the capacity to move us to judgement that this is good. There was recently the case of a father who was sent to prison for ten years for the cruel battering of his baby son. Who did not feel anger at that? And then, a few years ago, there was the case of the Penlee Life Boat, in which a whole crew of brave men, answering a call of a foundering ship on a night of howling storm, all gave their lives in an attempted rescue. The extent to which that moved people to something deeper than admiration, to something nearer a recognition that such action was profoundly good, was made plain by the national response to it. So value judgements are enormously important, because they enable us to choose between the good and the bad. And such judgements are, ultimately, made possible by the exercise of spiritual force.

But many other great things are inspired by the spiritual force. *The whole world of imagination*, linked with creativity, makes possible the worlds of science, art, literature, music and human relationships. All religious experience depends upon it. So it is of the highest importance to all of us to realise that this force exists, and to seek for it in the world around us and within our souls. Marcus Aurelius put it well when he said: 'Look well into yourself; there is a source which will always spring up if you will search there'.

Holy Spirit
But there is a particular manifestation of spiritual force which is of critical importance to the Christian experience and understanding of God. This is the operation of the Holy Spirit, whereby we are enabled to relate to God. Moral consciousness and religious aspiration are products of the work of this spirit. This is the Spirit of truth of which Jesus speaks

in St John's Gospel when, on the evening of the Last Supper, he was giving a farewell discourse to his disciples. 'When the Counsellor comes, whom I shall send to you from the Father, even the Spirit of truth, who proceeds from the Father, he will bear witness to me. . .'. (John 15.26). This was that which, as he promised, would be among them, a source of power, inspiration and guidance. It is the same spirit whose coming at the first Pentecost is described in Acts 2.1-4.

This is the famous account of how the Holy Spirit, making itself felt in the form of a great wind, startled the disciples as they were met together. It also filled them with power and joy, so that afterwards they were totally different people from what they had been. When Peter sought to explain to the people around what had happened, he quoted, significantly, from the prophet Joel; 'And in the last days it shall be, God declares, that I will pour out my spirit upon all flesh, and your sons and daughters shall prophesy, and young men shall see visions, and your old men shall dream dreams'. Here is a manifestation of that spiritual force which has vast implications and many applications. To limit the appearance of the Holy Spirit to this one manifestation at the first Pentecost, which has sometimes happened in Christian tradition, is to miss the truth that the Holy Spirit has a long history. The Spirit is the great fifth force in human experience, and the link between what happened at the first Pentecost and what is happening now whenever there is creativity present or value judgements, or imagination, or achievements in the highest order of art and literature and music and human relationships, is that all these things are signs of the manifold activities of this one and the same force. That which enables sons and daughters to prophecy and young men to see visions and old men to dream dreams is the same power whatever may be the content and the aim of the visions or the dreams. So there is evidence for the Spirit on all sides, provided we are prepared to look for it and to recognise it when we find it. There are five features to look for, five evidences of identity.

1. First is the *evidence of antiquity*. The Holy Spirit comes to us from a long past. When Peter addressed the crowd in Jerusalem at the first Pentecost he made this plain by quoting from the prophet Joel. The writers of the Old Testament knew from long experience about this Spirit. The New Testament continued the tradition, inherited the beliefs, and expanded them. 'Spirit' is the word used from the earliest times to denote the mysterious invisible power of God. It was present in the first days of creation when 'the spirit of God was moving over the face of the waters'. (Genesis 1.2). The Old Testament thinks of spirit also in terms of divine action operating like the wind, invisible, but with the power to change things, just as the desert wind was able mysteriously to alter the shape of the dunes. In the same manner the wind of the spirit, coming out of God's mysterious being, was able as they saw it, and as we can recognise it, to sweep across human lives, changing the shape of them, as God wills. Human life can be influenced and animated by this cosmic power of God. This spirit, is everywhere. 'Take not your holy Spirit from me' says the writer of Psalm 51, and 'where can I escape from your spirit?' asked the writer of Psalm 139. The writers of the New Testament saw the Holy Spirit as active in all kinds of areas, including artistic creation. When Moses was instructed by God to command the Tabernacle to be built he called upon craftsmen to help with the work who had been filled 'with ability to do every sort of work done by craftsmen or by a designer.' Essentially they had to be men 'in whose mind the Lord had put ability, everyone whose heart stirred him up to come to do the work. . .' (Exodus 36.2). In particular, the Old Testament writers recognised the spirit as that which inspired the prophets, seen not as so much as foretellers of the future, but as persons who were enabled to see into the heart of things and events and to speak the truth about them. Amos, a shepherd by occupation, became a prophet because God's spirit made him speak out. 'Surely the Lord God does nothing, without revealing his secret to his servants the prophets. The lion has roared; who will not fear? The Lord God has spoken; who can but prophesy?' (Amos 3. 7-8). The Holy Spirit is seen as also the power making for personal holiness and righteousness. This ties up with what we were thinking about spiritual force which enables people to make value judgements. So the writer of Psalm 51 says: 'Create in me a clean heart, O God, and put a new and right spirit within me'. (Psalm 51.10). And in a later age, as the Old Testament saw it, when messiah had come, there would be a great extension of the spirit's activities and power.

So in the New Testament evidence of the Holy Spirit is everywhere. The servant of the Lord, Christ himself, received the spirit at his baptism. (Mark 1.10). The first Christians believed that the old hope of the coming of one who had been anointed by the Spirit would be fulfilled in Jesus and that a wider spread of the power which Jesus promised would be with them and which did come upon them at Pentecost. Always, the mark of the inspiration of the Spirit has been shown in the quality and the character of true followers of Jesus. A gift of the Spirit is offered them: and if they receive it then they are baptized in the Spirit. St Paul was especially strong on this teaching. For example:

'But you are not in the flesh, you are in the Spirit, if in fact the Spirit of God really dwells in you. Any one who does not have the Spirit of Christ does not belong to him. But if Christ is in you, although your bodies are dead because of sin, your spirits are alive because of righteousness. If the Spirit of him who raised Jesus from the dead dwells in you, he who raised Christ Jesus from the dead will give life to your mortal bodies also through his Spirit which dwells in you'. (Romans 8.9-11).

So this spiritual force is something which is known about when it is experienced. Everybody moved by the Spirit has something to contribute to the well being of all, whatever his or her abilities and capabilities may be. And in all this, always, the New Testament is taking up the story of the Spirit and the evidences for the Spirit from the long past of man's experience of God.

2. A second identification to look for in searching for evidence of the Holy Spirit is that, like all sources of energy, *it acts with power*. Whenever the Spirit is mentioned in scripture something happens as a consequence. Where the Spirit of God is, there is God, and things happen. As we saw in the Old Testament, the primitive and fundamental idea of 'spirit' often denoted by the Hebrew word *ruahc*, is that of active power, superhuman, mysterious, of which the wind of the desert was a symbol. Significantly, Paul was thinking along similar lines when centuries later, speaking of Jesus, he said 'the Lord is the Spirit'. (2 Cor. 3.17). St John in his Gospel says 'God is spirit'. (John 4.24). So where God is present, he is always active, and he is active through his spirit. And this spirit is everywhere. 'Whither shall I go from thy Spirit, or whither shall I flee from thy presence?' asks the writer of Psalm 139.

When it became possible for people to have a new experience of God through Jesus Christ this sense of power emerges, especially in the conflict with powers of evil. The writers of the New Testament had no hesitation in seeing these powers as the demons of disease and insanity. Paul saw this spirit warfare waged against what he called principalities and powers. We in our day would do well to look around our world, notice its many darknesses and evils, and find in the power of the spirit that with which they may be faced.

The farewell address of Jesus to the Apostles in the upper room on the evening of the Last Supper before his arrest tells us a good deal more about this powerful spirit which will follow him. It will be unseen, and therefore unknown by the general world, but will be known to, and powerful in, the lives of the disciples of Christ. It will come in his name to teach and to bear witness to him. It will be given and sent by the father. This spirit is not independent of Christ's teaching but its complement. It derives from Christ itself, and opens the future to a service of him. It may therefore be said that where Christians act with power there is a spirit working within them, and, the opposite may be implied. And that leads to another identification mark of the Spirit.

3. This is that *the Holy Spirit is unpredictable*. There is an account of a happening in St John's Gospel which makes this very plain. A man called Nicodemus, distinguished and intelligent, came to Jesus one night – he did not want to be seen doing so by day – because he had a question to ask him. How could he find a way into that Kingdom of God of which he knew Jesus had been speaking? Jesus told him that there was no way other than that of being born again. Nicodemus asked: 'How can a man be born when he is old? Can he enter a second time into his mother's womb and be born?' Jesus replied:

Truly, truly, I say to you, unless one is born of water and the Spirit, he cannot enter the kingdom of God. That which is born of the flesh is flesh, and that which is born of the Spirit is spirit. Do not marvel that I said to you "You must be born anew". The wind blows where it wills, and you hear the sound of it, but you do not know whence it comes or whither it goes; so it is with every one who is born of the Spirit. (John 3.5-8).

He was saying, that this Spirit was unpredictable. It is impossible to say where or when or how it is going to operate. No one knows where it blows from. No one knows where it is blowing to. But everyone can see its power, as it alters the shape of things. As Nicodemus found, there are no neat and formal answers to anyone who wants experience of the Spirit. Recognition must always be given to the continuing fact that the Spirit is mysterious, cannot be planned, cannot be turned on and off. There is also another mark of identification.

4. *The spirit is a gift.* That is to say it comes from God. But it cannot be expected as a reward for piety or application. It is a gift which can be given to anybody, without regard to class, background, or intellectual power, as Amos the shepherd discovered, and as many have discovered since. That does not mean we can do nothing to bring this spirit into our own lives. The essential thing is to want this enlargement of the imagination, the understanding, the very soul, which the spirit brings. After that it is a matter of waiting, as the disciples waited at the first Pentecost, for this amazing, extraordinary, unpredictable, freely given power to descend upon one's life. If that spirit does descend upon the individual life, then certain very clearly indentifiable changes take place.

11

It can bring courage when courage is needed. When for instance Bishop Desmond Tutu in South Africa found himself suddenly faced with the need to pull a police informer out of a dangerous crowd, at the risk of life, he was able to do so. The Spirit can give people wonderful powers of endurance and patience. Some who are in a situation where they have to nurse a sick relative, husband, wife or child for years at a stretch often seem to be given a power of this kind.

5. *The Holy Spirit, has strong moral and ethical effects upon human conduct.* It changes people, their personalities and lifestyle. Evidence for this is to be found in all ages in people whose lives seem to have been motivated by some inspiration which has nothing to do with commonsense, or the desire to get on, or the wish to be famous, or the urge to achieve; but by something quite different – an overpowering desire to serve God through the service of people. A good instance of this in our days is Mother Teresa of Calcutta. What can be the drive behind a kind of life like that other than spiritual force? The same power can be found at work in many lives, however humble and obscure, where kindness and love seem to be the operating factors and where self-interest seems to count for very little. The common factor seems always to be this extra element which appears to have the ability both to strengthen the character and to enoble it.

St Paul summed up some of these changes which the Spirit can bring upon the human personality in a list of what he called the fruit of the Spirit: love, joy, peace, patience, kindness, goodness, fidelity, gentleness and self-control. He contrasted these with much of the human nature of his own day with its immorality, impurity, jealousies, envies, party spirit, dissensions, drunkenness. It sounds a pretty dire list; but who is to say that many of these things cannot be found in our own society now, reflected in the headlines and the news bulletins? The point is that the good qualities, the things which Paul calls the fruit of the Spirit, tend to come to those who, to use this phrase, 'walk by the Spirit', people who take their motivation from the Spirit rather than from the ways of the world. Love, for instance, is different from liking. Mother Teresa does not have to like the tattered and dirty remnants of humanity she finds upon the pavements of Calcutta; but, obviously, she does love them; and that is very different. And joy is an attitude of mind which is quite different from happiness. It does not in the least depend upon whether things are going well for us; but it depends entirely whether we can believe that God is with us, come what may. And peace does not mean the absence of war so much as an inner calm which comes from the capacity to believe that, because the world is God's, in the end, as Mother Julian of Norwich put it long ago, 'all shall be well'. And as to the other 'fruit' which Paul lists, it is worth asking whether one would like best to associate with someone who was patient, kind, and good, and faithful, and gentle, and self-controlled, rather than with someone who was not interested in these things at all. So, then, the spirit has the power to alter human nature for the better. J. B. Phillips summed it up well when he wrote: 'Every time we say "I believe in the Holy Spirit", we mean that we believe there is a living God able and willing to enter human personality and change it'.

A Summing Up

We began all this, looking at those great forces at work in the universe which science recognizes as governing the behaviour of matter: gravity, electro-magnetic force, the weak force, the strong force. All these, though of vast importance, are at the same time impersonal, not connected with human nature other than to the degree they affect the physical environment. But there is a fifth force, which profoundly affects human life, and that is spiritual, something so vast and varied that it touches upon human experience in many forms. Like the wind, it cannot be seen; but it can be perceived by what it does. It makes possible the worlds not only of science, but of religion, of art, literature, music and of human relationships. The evidence for this force is all around us. It is also to be found inside our own souls, or, as some prefer to say, within our own personalities. A Chinese philosopher, Hui Yuan, speaking of the need for self-fulfilment, spoke wisely when he said 'your treasure house is within. It contains all you will ever need. Use it fully, instead of seeking vainly outside yourself'.

But there was one particular manifestation of this spiritual force which is of critical importance to the Christian experience of God. This is the operation of the Holy Spirit, whereby we are enabled to relate to God. This is the Spirit of Truth of which Jesus speaks in St John's Gospel and which has acted with dramatic force throughout Christian history.

There are five ways in which this power can be recognised. First, in history, because the Holy Spirit has a long past, and we saw how it began in the minds of the writers of the Old Testament and how this was recognised by the writers of the New when they came to see the significance of their own experience in the light of it. Secondly, we saw that the Holy Spirit acts with power; thirdly, that it is unpredictable; fourthly, that it is a gift; and fifthly, that in its operation it has strong moral and ethical effects on human conduct. The evidence for the reality of spiritual force is to be found throughout human history. But, to anyone looking for these evidences, perhaps the best place to begin is within himself

14

or herself. It was Seneca, a philosopher of ancient Rome, who said long ago that 'God is near thee. He is with thee. He is within thee. There is no good man but hath God within him.'

But the great need is to recognise this truth, and to act upon it by receiving God into our lives. How is this to be done? By co-operating with his work, wherever all that is good and true is to be found, by putting ourselves in line with what he is doing, and so discovering his force and power. We are the work of God, just as are those forces we were thinking of, and by his spiritual force we can come to realise it and be inspired by it, and act accordingly.

Here are two prayers to help us, one old, from Samuel Johnson in the eighteenth century, one modern.

For the Guidance of the Holy Spirit

Enlighten our understandings with knowledge of right, and govern our wills by thy laws, that no deceit may mislead us, and no temptation corrupt us; that we may always endeavour to do good and hinder evil. Amid all the hopes and fears of this world, take not thy Holy Spirit from us.

Samuel Johnson 1709–84

★   ★   ★

Let us adore the Holy Spirit, who was there at creation, sweeping the emptiness, and bringing the universe from God's will to birth.
Spirit of God, powerful and unpredictable as the wind, you came upon the followers of Jesus at the first Pentecost and swept them off their feet, so that they found themselves

doing what they thought they never had it in them to do. . .
Spirit of God, come upon us and become the driving force of
our lives.

Contemporary Prayers, edited by Caryl Micklem

★   ★   ★

Acknowledgements and thanks are due to Dr G. H. Stafford, Master of St
Cross College, Oxford, for kindly contributing the section in this paper on
Material Forces.